CONVECTION OVEN COOKBOOK

MAIN COURSE – 80+ Quick and easy to prepare at home recipes, step-by-step guide to the best convection oven recipes

TABLE OF CONTENTS

BREAKFAST RECIPES 7

SHEPHERD'S PIE.. 7

MADELEINES.. 8

MORNING BLUEBERRIES 10

SUGAR FREE CUSTARD 11

WHOLE WHEAT EGG WHITE PUFF PANCAKE 12

OVEN FRIED EGGS 13

BAKED POTATO CASSEROLE 14

OIL-FREE CHIPOTLE FRIES 15

BAKED FRENCH TOAST 16

BREAKFAST OATMEAL COOKIES 18

MAPLE GRANOLA 19

DUTCH BABIES 20

SCOTCH EGGS 22

BLUEBERRY SCONES 23

APPLE CINNAMON SCONES 24

BREAKFAST BURRITOS 25

LEMON BREAD 27

CHINESE ALMOND COOKIES 28

DATE NUF LOAF... 29

COCONUT MILK AND CREAM 30

FRUIT BISCUITS.. 31

BREAKFAST CAKE RECIPES 33

EASY CARROT CAKE 33

CLASSIC POUND CAKE 34

STREUSEL COFFEE CAKE	35
ALMOND COFFE CAKE	37
PINEAPLLE CAKE	38
BALTIMORE CAKE	39
CHOCOLATE CAKE	40
CHOCOLATE CHIP COFFEE CAKE	42
BREAKFAST MUFFINS RECIPES	43
CINNAMON DONUT MUFFINS	43
PANCAKE MUFFINS	45
STARWBERRY OATMEAL MUFFINS	46
BANANA NUT MUFFINS	47
LUNCH	49
CHICKEN BREAST REUBEN	49
CHICKEN TORTILLA CUP	50
CHICKEN POT PIE	51
PLUM CHEESE CHICKEN	52
MEX TEX CHICKEN	53
SLOW COOKED FRIED CHICKEN	54
BAKED CHICKEN WINGS	55
ROASTED CHICKEN BREAST	56
BARBECUE CHICKEN	57
CHICKEN WITH VEGETABLES	58
LUNCH PIZZA RECIPES	60
PIZZA CRUST	60
VEGGIES PIZZA	61
GREEK FLATBREAD	62

FREND BREAD PIZZA 63

TROUT FILLET PACKETS 64

GARLIC CHICKEN WITH HERBS 65

PIZZA WITH BRUSSELS SPROUTS 66

SALAMI PIZZA 68

LOW CARB PIZZA 69

VEGAN PORTOBELLO PIZZA 70

ZUCCHINI PIZZA 71

GLUTEN FREE PIZZA 73

SOUS VIDE EGGS BENEDICT PIZZA 74

TUNA PIZZA 75

ARUGULA PIZZA 77

ENGLISH MUFFIN PIZZAS 78

CHIKEN PIZZA WITH GOAT CHEESE 79

ONION BACON PIZZA 80

POLENTA PIZZA 81

DINNER 83

FILO-WRAPPED BRIE 83

LAMB SHANKS WITH CAPERS 84

SICILIAN STRATA 85

SPICED TURKEY PICNIC LOAF 87

ROAST TURKEY 88

PECAN BALLS 89

ROASTED FISH 91

GREEK PEACH PIE 92

SPICED PECANS 93

BUTTERNUT SQUASH WITH TOMATOES	95
MAYONNAISE ROASTED TURKEY	96
BAKED SOWRDFISH	98
BEEF MEATBALLS	99
SALMON FILLETS	100
ROASTED MEAT AND VEGETABLES	101
CHEDDAR BACON EXPLOSION	102
FRENCH TOAST	103
ROASTED BACON	105

Copyright 2018 by Noah Jerris - All rights reserved.

This document is geared towards providing exact and reliable information in regards to the topic and issue covered. The publication is sold with the idea that the publisher is not required to render accounting, officially permitted, or otherwise, qualified services. If advice is necessary, legal or professional, a practiced individual in the profession should be ordered.

- From a Declaration of Principles which was accepted and approved equally by a Committee of the American Bar Association and a Committee of Publishers and Associations.

In no way is it legal to reproduce, duplicate, or transmit any part of this document in either electronic means or in printed format. Recording of this publication is strictly prohibited and any storage of this document is not allowed unless with written permission from the publisher. All rights reserved.

The information provided herein is stated to be truthful and consistent, in that any liability, in terms of inattention or otherwise, by any usage or abuse of any policies, processes, or directions contained within is the solitary and utter responsibility of the recipient reader. Under no circumstances will any legal responsibility or blame be held against the publisher for any reparation, damages, or monetary loss due to the information herein, either directly or indirectly.

Respective authors own all copyrights not held by the publisher.

The information herein is offered for informational purposes solely, and is universal as so. The presentation of the information is without contract or any type of guarantee assurance.

The trademarks that are used are without any consent, and the publication of the trademark is without permission or backing by the trademark owner. All trademarks and brands within this book are for clarifying purposes only and are the owned by the owners themselves, not affiliated with this document.

Introduction

Convection oven recipes for family enjoyment. You will love them for sure for how easy it is to prepare them.

BREAKFAST RECIPES

SHEPHERD'S PIE

Serves: *8*

Prep Time: *10* Minutes

Cook Time: *40* Minutes

Total Time: *50* Minutes

INGREDIENTS

- ½ cup carrots
- ½ cup celery
- ½ cup onion
- ½ cup green onion
- 3 cloves garlic
- 1 cup shiitake mushrooms
- 1 cup edamame
- ½ cup white wine
- 1 lb. leftover turkey meat
- 3 cups gravy
- ¼ cup soy sauce
- 1 tsp sesame oil
- 4 cups mashed potatoes
- 1 tablespoon olive oil

DIRECTIONS

1. Preheat convection oven to 400 F
2. In a pot sauté the vegetables and add wine while cooking
3. Fold in the turkey meat, add gravy, soy sauce, sesame oil and taste the mixture
4. Spoon the filling into a casserole dish, top with mashed potatoes, bake for 30 minutes and turn the fan to the convection oven
5. When ready, remove let it cool and serve

MADELEINES

Serves: **12**

Prep Time: **10** Minutes

Cook Time: **30** Minutes

Total Time: **40** Minutes

INGREDIENTS

- ½ cup all purpose flour
- ½ tsp baking powder
- ½ tsp salt
- 1 tsp honey

- 1 drop lemon oil
- ½ cup eggs
- 2/4 cup granulated sugar
- 2-ounces butter
- 1 tsp brown sugar

DIRECTIONS

1. In a bowl add salt, baking powder flour and whisk together
2. In another bowl mix sugar, eggs and use an electric mixer to mix for 3-4 minutes
3. In a saucepan heat butter, add honey, brown sugar and cook for 1-2 minutes
4. Remove the bowl from the mixer and fold in the dry ingredients and mix well
5. Pour the butter over the batter, add lemon oil and refrigerate
6. Brush the madeleine pan with butter, transfer the batter into molds and bake in the convection oven for 9-10 minute
7. When ready, remove and serve

MORNING BLUEBERRIES

Serves: **8**

Prep Time: **10** Minutes

Cook Time: **60** Minutes

Total Time: **70** Minutes

INGREDIENTS

- 1 cup frozen blueberries
- 1 cup water
- 1 cup salt

DIRECTIONS

1. In a saucepan simmer blueberries and water over medium heat for 5-6 minutes and set aside
2. Smash the blueberries with a spoon and line them on a baking sheet
3. Return the remaining juice from the blueberries to a saucepan and boil until reduced to a syrup
4. Spread over the baking sheets and let it dry for a couple of hours
5. Bake at 175 F for 1 hour

SUGAR FREE CUSTARD

Serves: **4**

Prep Time: **10** Minutes

Cook Time: **30** Minutes

Total Time: **40** Minutes

INGREDIENTS

- 3 cups 1% milk
- 3 eggs
- ½ cup Splenda
- 1 tsp vanilla
- dash of grated nutmeg
- 4 cups ramicans
- 1-quart hot water

DIRECTIONS

1. In a bowl pour milk and microwave for 1-2 minutes
2. In another bowl beat eggs and pour milk into the bowl and whisk, add vanilla and Splenda
3. In the pan place the ramicans, and pour the hot mixture into the cups

4. Place the pan into the oven and pour hot water into the pan with ramicans
5. Bake for 30 minutes at 300 F in the convection oven
6. When ready remove and serve

WHOLE WHEAT EGG WHITE PUFF PANCAKE

Serves: **4**

Prep Time: **10** Minutes

Cook Time: **30** Minutes

Total Time: **40** Minutes

INGREDIENTS

- ½ cup egg whites
- ½ cup almond milk
- ½ cup wheat pastry flour
- ½ tablespoon flaxseed meal
- ½ tsp vanilla extract
- ½ tsp stevia
- 1 tsp frozen berries

DIRECTIONS

1. In a blend add all ingredients except berries and blend until smooth, when ready add berries
2. Pour mixture into ramekin and bake for 35 minutes at 325 F or until ready
3. When ready, remove and serve

OVEN FRIED EGGS

Serves: *4*

Prep Time: *10* Minutes

Cook Time: *10* Minutes

Total Time: *20* Minutes

INGREDIENTS

- 4-5 eggs
- 1 tablespoon coconut oil
- salt

DIRECTIONS

1. Preheat convection oven to 375 F
2. Into an iron cast add oil

3. Crack the eggs into the mixing bowl and place them into the iron cast
4. Bake for a couple of minutes, 6-7 minutes or until done
5. Remove eggs from the oven, sprinkle salt and serve

BAKED POTATO CASSEROLE

Serves: **4**

Prep Time: **10** Minutes

Cook Time: **30** Minutes

Total Time: **40** Minutes

INGREDIENTS

- 2 lbs. baking potatoes
- ½ cup milk
- 1 tsp salt
- 1 tsp black pepper
- 2 cups shredded cheese
- 10 strips bacon
- ½ cup green onions
- ½ cup butter

- 1/3 cup soar cream

DIRECTIONS

1. Preheat convection oven to 400 F and pierce each potato and place them on a baking dish
2. Bake for 45-50 minutes or until tender, remove and let them cool
3. When potatoes are done reduce temperature to 325
4. In a bowl add butter, pepper, sour cream, milk, salt and stir to combine
5. Add cheese, green onions, bacon and stir to combine
6. Spray a casserole with cooking spray and turn the potato mixture out into dish
7. Sprinkle with cheese and onions and bake for 20-30 minutes
8. Remove and serve

OIL-FREE CHIPOTLE FRIES

Serves: 2
Prep Time: 15 Minutes
Cook Time: 25 Minutes
Total Time: 40 Minutes

INGREDIENTS

- 4 potatoes
- dried chipotle pepper
- salt / pepper
- juice from 1 lemon

DIRECTIONS

1. Preheat convection oven to 400 F
2. Slice the potatoes and in a bowl toss them in lemon juice and sprinkle with pepper
3. Spread the potatoes on a baking sheet and sprinkle with more pepper and bake for 15 minutes, flip them and bake for another 10 minutes or until golden brown, remove and serve

BAKED FRENCH TOAST

Serves: **4**

Prep Time: **10** Minutes

Cook Time: **50** Minutes

Total Time: **60** Minutes

INGREDIENTS

- 6 eggs
- 1 cup milk
- 5 tablespoons brown sugar
- 1 tsp cinnamon
- ½ tsp salt
- 1 tablespoon vanilla extract
- 1 lb. French bread

TOPPING

- 4 tablespoons brown sugar
- 3 tablespoons white sugar
- ½ tsp cinnamon
- ½ tsp nutmeg
- 1 tablespoon butter

DIRECTIONS

1. Into a bowl crack eggs and whisk to combine, add cinnamon, salt, vanilla and brown sugar
2. Cut bread into chunks, whisk egg mixture and pour evenly over bread
3. Spread out evenly and place in fridge overnight
4. In another bowl mix all topping ingredients, cover and place in fridge overnight
5. Preheat oven to 325 F, sprinkle topping over top and bake for 45 minutes or until golden brown
6. When ready remove and serve

BREAKFAST OATMEAL COOKIES

Serves: **12**

Prep Time: **10** Minutes

Cook Time: **10** Minutes

Total Time: **20** Minutes

INGREDIENTS

- ½ cup margarine
- ¼ AP flour
- 1 tsp baking soda
- 1 tsp cinnamon
- ¾ cup brown sugar
- ½ tsp salt
- ¼ tsp clove
- 1 cup rolled oats
- 2/4 cup pecan pieces
- 1 cup chocolate chips
- 1 tsp vanilla
- 2 eggs
- 1 cup wheat flour
- ½ tsp nutmeg

DIRECTIONS

1. Preheat convection oven to 325 F
2. In a bowl mix salt, vanilla, brown sugar and margarine and beat well for 2-3 minutes
3. Add eggs and continue to beat
4. In another bowl mix baking soda, cinnamon, nutmeg, flours, and clove, mix well and add all in a single bowl and mix well
5. Prepare cookie sheets, pour ¼ cup measure on the baking sheets and make 12 cookies
6. Book for 5-10 minutes or until golden brown
7. Remove and serve

MAPLE GRANOLA

Serves: 8
Prep Time: 10 Minutes
Cook Time: 40 Minutes
Total Time: 50 Minutes

INGREDIENTS

- 12 cups oats

- 3 tsp vanilla extract
- 2 tsp salt
- 2 cups dried fruit
- 1 cup almonds
- 1 cup pecan
- 2 cups maple syrup

DIRECTIONS

1. Preheat convection oven to 275 and pour oats and nuts in a bowl
2. In a pot heat maple syrup and salt and stir in vanilla extract
3. Pour maple syrup mixture over oats and nuts, stir in oats
4. Pour batter on baking sheets and bake for 35 minutes or until golden brown
5. Remove and let it cool before serving

DUTCH BABIES

Serves: **6**
Prep Time: **10** Minutes
Cook Time: **20** Minutes

Total Time: *30* Minutes

INGREDIENTS

- 5 eggs
- ½ tsp salt
- 1 cup flour
- 2 tablespoons sugar
- 1 tsp vanilla
- ½ tsp cinnamon
- 1 cup milk

DIRECTIONS

1. Preheat oven to 425 F
2. In a bowl mix all ingredients
3. In a pan toss a couple tablespoons of butter
4. Pull the pan back out and pour all the batter in and slide it in the oven for 15-20 minutes
5. Cook until golden brown, remove and serve

SCOTCH EGGS

Serves: **2**

Prep Time: **10** Minutes

Cook Time: **20** Minutes

Total Time: **30** Minutes

INGREDIENTS

- 3 eggs
- 3 toothpicks
- 1 package pork sausage
- 6 slices cut bacon

DIRECTIONS

1. Hard boil the eggs
2. Split the sausage into 4 equal parts
3. Place an egg into each circle and wrap it with the sausage
4. Refrigerate for 45 minutes
5. Make a cross with 2 slices of bacon and place a wrapped egg in the center and fold the bacon over top of the egg
6. Cook at 420 F for 20 minutes

BLUEBERRY SCONES

Serves: *8*

Prep Time: *10* Minutes

Cook Time: *20* Minutes

Total Time: *30* Minutes

INGREDIENTS

- 2 cups flour
- ½ tsp vanilla
- 1 cup blueberries
- 1 tsp salt
- 2 tablespoons sugar
- 1 cup yogurt
- 1 tablespoon sugar
- 1 tablespoon baking powder
- ½ tsp baking soda

DIRECTIONS

1. Preheat convection oven to 350 F
2. Mix dry ingredients add, yogurt and vanilla and mix until all incorporated
3. Add blueberries, fold in until well distributed

4. Place dough on a baking pad, cut into 8 wedges and separate them
5. Dust with sugar and transfer to the oven and bake for 20 minutes, remove and serve

APPLE CINNAMON SCONES

Serves: **8**

Prep Time: **10** Minutes

Cook Time: **20** Minutes

Total Time: **30** Minutes

INGREDIENTS

- 1 apple
- ½ cup milk
- 5 tablespoons butter
- 1 cup AP flour
- 1 tsp cinnamon
- 1 egg
- ½ cup sugar
- 1 tsp baking powder
- ½ tsp baking soda

- ½ tsp salt

TOPPING

- 1 tablespoon sugar
- 1 tsp cinnamon

DIRECTIONS

1. Preheat convection oven to 375 F
2. Chop a couple of tablespoons of butter
3. In a bowl add baking powder, baking soda, AP flour, sugar, salt, cinnamon, add butter and mix well
4. Add milk, one egg and mix well
5. Add the egg mixture to the dry mixture and mix until fully incorporated, add apple and mix
6. Place on a floured surface and into into 8 wedges
7. In a bowl mix sugar with cinnamon and place wedges on a cooking sheet
8. Top with cinnamon mixture and place in the convection oven and cook for 15-20 minutes or until golden brown, remove and serve

BREAKFAST BURRITOS

Serves: **40**
Prep Time: **10** Minutes

Cook Time: *30*   Minutes

Total Time: *40*   Minutes

INGREDIENTS

- 40 eggs
- 2 lbs. turkey
- 10-ounces green bell peppers
- 12-ounces onions
- 1 fresh tomato
- ¼ cup mustard
- 1 tsp garlic
- 1 tablespoon pepper sauce
- 1 cup corn
- 2/4 cup fat milk
- 1 tsp salt
- 40 flour tortillas
- 2 lbs. salsa

DIRECTIONS

1. In a bowl mix green peppers, eggs, ham, corn, milk, turkey, onions, mustard, tomatoes, garlic salt and pepper sauce and using a mixer mix well
2. Pour egg mixture into a steam table pan
3. Bake at 300 F for 45 minutes
4. Fill each tortilla with 10 scoop of cook egg mixture, roll tortilla and serve with salsa

LEMON BREAD

Serves: *8*

Prep Time: *10* Minutes

Cook Time: *20* Minutes

Total Time: *30* Minutes

INGREDIENTS

- 1 cup sugar
- 1 tsp baking powder
- 1 tsp salt
- ½ cup milk
- 1/3 cup butter
- 1 tsp lemon extract
- ¼ cup lemon juice
- 1 egg
- 1 cup all-purpose flour

DIRECTIONS

1. In a bowl mix butter, juice and sugar and beat eggs until smooth
2. In another bowl mix baking powder, salt and flour, stir in wet ingredients and add milk

3. Add pecans, lemon and pour batter into a loaf pan
4. Bake at 325 F for 60 minutes in the convection oven
5. Remove and pour topping over the bread (dissolve sugar in lemon juice), pour topping over crust

CHINESE ALMOND COOKIES

Serves: *8*

Prep Time: *10* Minutes

Cook Time: *20* Minutes

Total Time: *30* Minutes

INGREDIENTS

- 2 cups flour
- ½ tsp salt
- 1 cup sugar
- 1 egg
- ½ cup almonds
- ½ tsp soda
- 1 cup butter
- 1 tsp almond extract

DIRECTIONS

1. In a bowl sift sugar, soda, salt and flour
2. Cut in butter, add egg, almond extract and mix well
3. Shape dough into 1 inch balls and place on a cookie sheet
4. Bake at 300 F for 20 minutes
5. Remove and serve

DATE NUF LOAF

Serves: *6*

Prep Time: *10* Minutes

Cook Time: *20* Minutes

Total Time: *30* Minutes

INGREDIENTS

- 8 oz. coconut
- 2 tablespoons vanilla
- 1 can condensed milk
- 6 oz. chopped dates
- 2 cups pecans

DIRECTIONS

1. In a bowl mix all ingredients
2. Bake at 325 F for 35 minutes
3. Remove and serve

COCONUT MILK AND CREAM

Serves: **4**
Prep Time: **10** Minutes

Cook Time: **30** Minutes

Total Time: **40** Minutes

INGREDIENTS

- 1 coconut

MILK

- 2 oz. grated coconut
- ½ cup boiling milk

CREAM

- 4 oz. grated coconut
- ½ cup boiling milk

DIRECTIONS

1. Preheat oven to 350 F and place coconut into a bowl
2. Turn the coconut upside down over a container and drain the water and store in a refrigerator
3. Place the coconut onto a sheet pan and bake for 15 minutes
4. Rinse the coconut meat under cool water and pat dry
5. For milk, place 2 ounces of the coconut into a mixing bowl and pour over the boiling milk, transfer mixture to a blender and blend until smooth
6. For the cream, repeat the same process

FRUIT BISCUITS

Serves: 8

Prep Time: 10 Minutes

Cook Time: 15 Minutes

Total Time: 25 Minutes

INGREDIENTS

- 1 oz. biscuits
- ½ cup melted butter

- ½ cup sugar
- ½ tsp cinnamon
- 8 tablespoons raspberry or strawberry preserves

DIRECTIONS

1. Preheat oven to 350 F
2. Dip both sides of biscuits into melted butter and then into cinnamon and sugar
3. Fill the center of each biscuit with fruit preserves
4. Arrange biscuits on a baking sheet and bake for 12-15 minutes or until golden brown
5. Remove and serve

BREAKFAST CAKE RECIPES

EASY CARROT CAKE

Serves: **6**

Prep Time: **10** Minutes

Cook Time: **40** Minutes

Total Time: **50** Minutes

INGREDIENTS

- 1 box cake mix
- 1 cup grated carrots
- ½ cup water
- 2 eggs
- ½ cup vegetable oil
- ½ cup raisins
- ¼ cup pineapple
- 1 tsp cinnamon
- ½ cup walnuts

DIRECTIONS

1. Preheat convection oven to 325 F
2. Brush a cake pan with butter and flour

3. In a bowl add all the ingredients and beat on low speed until everything is incorporated
4. Divided the batter into 2 pans and bake for 35 minutes
5. Remove and allow cakes to cook and serve

CLASSIC POUND CAKE

Serves: *8*
Prep Time: *10* Minutes
Cook Time: *30* Minutes
Total Time: *40* Minutes

INGREDIENTS

- 1 cup sugar
- 5 eggs
- ½ cup buttermilk
- 2 cups all-purpose flour
- 1 tsp salt
- 1 tsp vanilla extract
- 1 cup unsalted butter
- 3 tsp baking powder

DIRECTIONS

1. Preheat oven to 300 F
2. In a bowl mix butter and sugar using an electric mixer
3. Add eggs and stream in the buttermilk slowly
4. Incorporate the dry ingredients and mix until fully incorporated
5. Transfer to a loaf pan and bake for 20 minutes
6. Remove from the convection oven and serve with ice cream

STREUSEL COFFEE CAKE

Serves: *8*

Prep Time: *10* Minutes

Cook Time: *25* Minutes

Total Time: *35* Minutes

INGREDIENTS

- ½ cup sugar
- ½ cup AP flour
- 2 tablespoons butter
- ½ tsp cinnamon

WET INGREDIENTS
- 2/4 cup milk
- ½ cup oil
- 1 egg

DRY INGREDIENTS
- 1 cup AP flour
- ½ cup white sugar
- 1 tablespoons baking powder
- ¼ tsp salt
- ½ tsp cinnamon

DIRECTIONS

1. Preheat oven to 350 F and spray a baking pan with butter
2. In a bow mix butter, brown sugar, cinnamon and flour
3. Into a mix all dry ingredients
4. In another bowl mix all wet ingredients
5. Combine wet and dry ingredients and mix well
6. Pour batter into prepared pan and top with brown sugar mixture
7. Bake for 25 minutes or until golden brown, remove and serve

ALMOND COFFE CAKE

Serves: **4**

Prep Time: **10** Minutes

Cook Time: **40** Minutes

Total Time: **50** Minutes

INGREDIENTS

- 1 apple
- ½ cup brown sugar
- ½ cup almonds
- ½ cup raisins
- 1 egg
- 1 cup flour
- 1 tsp baking soda
- 1 tsp cinnamon
- 1 tsp allspice
- ½ tsp cardamom
- ½ tsp salt
- ½ cup butter
- 1 tsp vanilla extract

DIRECTIONS

1. Toss apples with sugar, raisins and almonds
2. In a bowl beat eggs mix with vanilla, butter and stir into apple mixture
3. In another bowl mix salt, cardamom, flour, baking soda, cinnamon and all spice
4. Stir dry ingredients into apple mixture
5. Spoon into a baking and bake at 350 F for 40 minutes
6. Remove and serve

PINEAPLLE CAKE

Serves: **6**
Prep Time: **10** Minutes

Cook Time: **20** Minutes

Total Time: **30** Minutes

INGREDIENTS

- 2 cup all-purpose flour
- ¼ tsp salt
- 20 oz. can crushed pineapple
- 1 cup sugar
- 1 tsp baking soda

TOPPING

- ¾ cup brown sugar
- 1 can milk
- 1 butter
- 2/4 cup sugar
- ¾ cup pecans

DIRECTIONS

1. Mix all ingredients and pour into a greased pan
2. Sprinkle with brown sugar and pecans
3. Bake at 325 F for 35 minutes
4. In a bowl mix all topping ingredients
5. Boil for 5-10 minutes and pour over cake

BALTIMORE CAKE

Serves: **6**

Prep Time: **10** Minutes

Cook Time: **20** Minutes

Total Time: **30** Minutes

INGREDIENTS

- 2 cup cake flour
- 3 tsp baking powder
- 1 tsp salt
- 2/3 cup vegetable shortening
- 1 cup sugar
- 1 cup milk
- 1 tsp vanilla
- 3 egg whites

DIRECTIONS

1. In a bowl mix sugar, flour, baking powder, salt, milk and stir in vanilla
2. Beat at low speed with electric mixer for 2-3 minutes and add remaining milk and egg whites
3. Pour the cake batter into the prepared pans
4. Bake at 325 F for 30 minutes, remove and serve

CHOCOLATE CAKE

Serves: *6*
Prep Time: *15* Minutes
Cook Time: *30* Minutes

Total Time: 45 Minutes

INGREDIENTS

I1

- ½ cup sugar
- 1/3 cup cocoa
- ½ cup water

I2

- ½ shortening
- 1 slice sugar
- 1 egg
- 1 tsp soda
- 1/3 tsp salt
- ½ cup water
- 2 cups cake flour
- ½ tsp vanilla

DIRECTIONS

1. Mix all ingredients from I1 and bring to boil
2. Cream shortening, add sugar and beat until smooth
3. Beat eggs, add salt, flour and soda
4. Add dry ingredients with vanilla, combine with first mixture
5. Pour into two layer pans, greased with flour
6. Bake at 325 F for 30 minutes
7. Remove and serve

CHOCOLATE CHIP COFFEE CAKE

Serves: 5

Prep Time: *10* Minutes

Cook Time: *40* Minutes

Total Time: *50* Minutes

INGREDIENTS

I1

- 1 cup dates chopped
- 1 cup boiling water
- 1 tsp

I2

- 2 cup butter
- 1 cup sugar
- 1 egg
- 1 tsp vanilla
- 1 cup flour
- ½ tsp baking soda

I3

- 3 cup brown sugar
- ½ cup walnuts
- 1 cup chocolate chips

DIRECTIONS

1. In a bowl mix dates with boiling water and soda
2. Cream butter and sugar together and add eggs and vanilla
3. Add soda and flour
4. Add date mixture and pour into a greased pan
5. Sprinkle with ingredients form I3 and bake for 40 minutes at 325 F

BREAKFAST MUFFINS RECIPES

CINNAMON DONUT MUFFINS

Serves: **10**
Prep Time: **10** Minutes
Cook Time: **20** Minutes
Total Time: **30** Minutes

INGREDIENTS

- 1 cup all-purpose organic flour
- 1 tsp baking powder
- ½ tsp salt

- ½ tsp nutmeg
- ½ tsp cinnamon
- 1/3 cup butter
- 1/3 cup sugar
- 1 egg
- 2/4 cup milk

COATING

- ½ cup butter
- ¾ cup sugar
- 1 tsp cinnamon

DIRECTIONS

1. Preheat convection oven to325 F
2. In a bowl mix all dry ingredients and set aside
3. In another bowl mix all wet ingredients
4. Add wet ingredients to dry ingredients and stir to combine
5. Distribute batter into 10 muffin cups
6. For coating mix cinnamon and sugar
7. Bake for 20 minutes
8. Remove and serve

PANCAKE MUFFINS

Serves: **8**

Prep Time: **10** Minutes

Cook Time: **15** Minutes

Total Time: **25** Minutes

INGREDIENTS

- Mixed pancake batter
- Oil
- Mini muffin pan
- Toppings: chocolate chips, berries, cinnamon

DIRECTIONS

1. Preheat convection oven to 325 F and grease muffin pans
2. Prepare pancake batter
3. Fill muffin cups with pancake batter and add toppings
4. Bake for 12-15 minutes or until golden brown
5. Remove and serve

STARWBERRY OATMEAL MUFFINS

Serves: **12**

Prep Time: **10** Minutes

Cook Time: **15** Minutes

Total Time: **25** Minutes

INGREDIENTS

- 1 cup oats
- 1 cup buttermilk
- 1 cup all-purpose milk
- ½ tsp salt
- 1 tsp baking powder
- ½ cup brown sugar
- 1 egg
- ½ cup oil
- 1 tsp vanilla extract
- ½ tsp cinnamon
- 1 cup strawberries

DIRECTIONS

1. Preheat your convection oven to 400 F

2. In a bowl mix buttermilk and oats and soak for 12-15 minutes
3. In another bowl whisk tougher baking soda, baking powder, flour, cinnamon and salt
4. Stir in egg, oil, vanilla, sugar into oat mixture and add dry ingredients and stir

BANANANUT MUFFINS

Serves: *12*

Prep Time: *10* Minutes

Cook Time: *20* Minutes

Total Time: *30* Minutes

INGREDIENTS

WET

- 2 bananas ripe
- 1 egg
- ½ cup butter
- 2 tablespoons coffee
- 1 tsp vanilla

DRY

- 1 cup AL flour

- ¾ cup sugar
- ½ cup walnuts
- 1 tsp salt
- 1 tsp baking powder
- ½ tsp baking soda
- ½ tsp cinnamon
- ½ nutmeg

DIRECTIONS

1. Preheat convection oven to 325 and mash the bananas
2. Melt butter in the microwave
3. Add one egg to the banana and mix well, add butter, vanilla, coffee, milk
4. Mix walnuts with sugar, baking powder, AP flour, baking soda, nutmeg and cinnamon
5. Mix wet ingredients with dry ingredients until well incorporated
6. Pour batter into 12 cupcake baking cups sprinkle with sugar and bake for 20 minutes
7. Remove and serve

LUNCH

CHICKEN BREAST REUBEN

Serves: *4*

Prep Time: *10* Minutes

Cook Time: *20* Minutes

Total Time: *30* Minutes

INGREDIENTS

- 1 cup pesto
- 1 chicken breast
- 1 package 16 oz. corned beef
- 3 slice Swiss cheese
- 3 French bread rolls
- 1 can 14 can sauerkraut

DIRECTIONS

1. Split chicken breast and place it on a baking pan and bake for 20 minutes at 175 F
2. Spread pesto on the chicken breast
3. Add beef, sauerkraut, Swiss cheese and serve with salad

CHICKEN TORTILLA CUP

Serves: **6**

Prep Time: **10** Minutes

Cook Time: **40** Minutes

Total Time: **50** Minutes

INGREDIENTS

- 5 corn tortillas
- 1 tablespoon cilantro
- 5 tablespoons red bell pepper
- salt
- 2 cup cooked chicken
- 1 cup chopped tomatoes
- 1 white onion

DIRECTIONS

1. Oil the cups of a muffin tin, push tortillas into muffin cups
2. Bake for 35 minutes, remove and let it cool
3. In a bowl mix remaining ingredients and season with salt
4. Serve when ready

CHICKEN POT PIE

Serves: *4*

Prep Time: *10* Minutes

Cook Time: *20* Minutes

Total Time: *30* Minutes

INGREDIENTS

- 1 can chicken
- 1 sage leaves
- salt
- 2 frozen pie crusts
- 1 can mixed vegetables
- 1 can cream of chicken soup

DIRECTIONS

1. In a bowl mix all ingredients
2. Place mixture into pie crust and top with the second pie crust
3. Bake in the convection oven for 20 minutes at 300 F or until done
4. Remove and serve

PLUM CHEESE CHICKEN

Serves: **4**

Prep Time: **10** Minutes

Cook Time: **30** Minutes

Total Time: **40** Minutes

INGREDIENTS

- 3 boneless chicken breasts
- 6 oz. cream cheese
- 1 tablespoon plum jam
- 2 dashed garlic powder
- ½ cup melted butter
- toasted bread crumbs

DIRECTIONS

1. Pound chicken until thin, sprinkle with pepper, salt and garlic powder
2. Mix with plum jam, cream cheese, garlic powder and spread on chicken breast
3. Dip each chicken breast in melted butter and then roll in bread crumbs
4. Bake at 325 F for 30 minutes, remove and serve

MEX TEX CHICKEN

Serves: *4*
Prep Time: *10* Minutes
Cook Time: *30* Minutes
Total Time: *40* Minutes

INGREDIENTS

- 2 can cream of mushroom soup
- 1 can rotel with ½ can water
- 2 chicken breasts diced
- 1 large bag doritoes
- 1 bag shredded cheese

DIRECTIONS

1. In a bowl mix 2 cans of cream of mushroom soup with rotel and ½ can water
2. Pour soup mixture and rotel in a casserole, cut chicken and put in casserole and mix well
3. Sprinkle with crushed doritoes and cheese
4. Bake at 325 F for 30 minutes, remove and serve

SLOW COOKED FRIED CHICKEN

Serves: **4**

Prep Time: **20** Minutes

Cook Time: **150** Minutes

Total Time: **170** Minutes

INGREDIENTS

- 4 lbs. chicken wings
- ½ cup sugar
- 1 tablespoon honey
- 4 cloves garlic peeled
- black pepper
- 8 oz. soy sauce
- ½ cup brown sugar

DIRECTIONS

1. In a blender add sugar, honey, molasses, soy sauce, pepper, garlic and ginger and blend until smooth
2. In pan place the frozen chicken and pour blended mixture
3. Bake at 275 F for 150 minutes and turn every 30 minutes, cook until tender

4. Remove from convection oven and serve

BAKED CHICKEN WINGS

Serves: **4**

Prep Time: **20** Minutes

Cook Time: **40** Minutes

Total Time: **60** Minutes

INGREDIENTS

- 1 can coconut milk
- salt
- 8 chicken drumbsticks
- 1 cup bread crumbs
- ½ tablespoon goya seasoning
- 1 tablespoon mustard

DIRECTIONS

1. In a bowl mix paprika, mustard, milk and mix well, add drumsticks and let it stand for 20-30 minutes
2. Preheat oven to 375 F

3. Add goya seasoning and season chicken with pepper and salt
4. Cook for 40 minutes, remove and serve

ROASTED CHICKEN BREAST

Serves: 2
Prep Time: 10 Minutes
Cook Time: 50 Minutes
Total Time: 60 Minutes

INGREDIENTS

- 2 oz. chicken breasts
- 2 slice bacon
- ½ tsp Italian herb
- salt

DIRECTIONS

1. Heat oven to 350 and line a baking sheet
2. Sprinkle breast with salt, Italian herb and pepper
3. Law two slices of bacon over each breast and bake for 40 minutes at 160 F

4. Cut bacon into pieces, remove breasts from bone and sprinkle with bacon pieces

BARBECUE CHICKEN

Serves: **4**

Prep Time: **10** Minutes

Cook Time: **100** Minutes

Total Time: **110** Minutes

INGREDIENTS

- ¼ cup apple cider vinegar
- ½ cup water
- ½ tsp salt
- ½ tsp cayenne
- 1 tablespoon mustard
- ½ tsp pepper
- 1 tablespoon Worcestershire sauce
- 1 tsp liquid smoke
- 1 whole chicken
- ½ cup butter
- ½ cup ketchup
- 1 clove garlic

- 1 onion
- 1 tablespoon sugar

DIRECTIONS

1. Preheat convection oven to 300 F
2. In a saucepan mix apple vinegar,
3. Water, salt, cayenne, garlic, onion, brown sugar, mustard, pepper, butter and cook for 15-20 minutes
4. Add ketchup and Worcestershire sauce and mix well
5. Place chicken in a pan and pour half the sauce
6. Place the pan in the convection oven and bake for 90 minutes, remove and serve

CHICKEN WITH VEGETABLES

Serves: **6**
Prep Time: **10** Minutes

Cook Time: **60** Minutes

Total Time: **70** Minutes

INGREDIENTS

- 2 frying chickens

- 2 tablespoons butter
- salt and pepper

VEGETABLES

- 1 cup water
- 1 tsp beef bouillon
- 1 cup green onion
- 14 oz. chestnuts
- ½ cup pineapple juice
- 2 tsp cornstarch
- 1 tablespoon soy sauce
- 1 cup sliced celery
- 1 cup sliced carrots
- 1 cup green peppers

DIRECTIONS

1. Coat chicken with flour, melt butter in a baking dish and place the chicken in it
2. Bake at 375 F for 20 minutes and then reduce heat to 325 and bake for another 35 minutes or until tender
3. For vegetables mix water, beef bouillon, soy sauce and celery and bring to boil
4. Reduce heat and add green pepper, carrots, celery and boil for another 5-6 minutes
5. Add green onion, water and cook for another 2-3 minutes
6. Remove vegetables to a plate, add pineapple juice, cornstarch and stir into broth
7. Pour over vegetables and serve

LUNCH PIZZA RECIPES

PIZZA CRUST

Serves: 2
Prep Time: 10 Minutes
Cook Time: 10 Minutes
Total Time: 20 Minutes

INGREDIENTS

- 3 cups flour
- ½ cup water
- 1 package dry yeast
- ½ tsp salt
- 1 tablespoon olive oil

DIRECTIONS

1. Boil water and dissolve ¼ cup of yeast and set aside
2. In bowl mix, olive oil, 2 cups flour, salt to make the dough and stir in yeast and remaining flour
3. Place in a bowl and let rise for about 4-5 minutes
4. Divide into 2 balls and roll out to make 2 pizzas
5. Top with toppings and bake at 300 F or until bubbly

6. **Remove and serve**

VEGGIES PIZZA

Serves: 2

Prep Time: **10**   Minutes

Cook Time: **20**   Minutes

Total Time: **30**   Minutes

INGREDIENTS

- 2 homemade pizza crusts
- 1 onion
- 2 tomatoes sliced
- 1 bunch basil
- 1 bunch chives
- 1 clove garlic
- 1 cup homemade pizza sauce
- ½ cup olive oil
- shredded mozzarella cheese

DIRECTIONS

1. **Drizzle pizza crust with olive oil and add sauce**

2. Add tomatoes, garlic and onion, basil and chives
3. Top with mozzarella cheese
4. Bake at 325 F for 20 minute or until golden brown

GREEK FLATBREAD

Serves: **4**

Prep Time: **10** Minutes

Cook Time: **30** Minutes

Total Time: **40** Minutes

INGREDIENTS

- 2 pieces of flatbread
- 1 piece of leftover chicken
- 2 tablespoons leftover peas
- 1 tomato
- ½ cup parmesan cheese
- 2 tsp olive oil
- 2 tablespoons Greek yogurt
- 2 dashed onion powder

DIRECTIONS

1. Over the flatbread drizzle olive oil and spread Greek yogurt
2. Sprinkle, garlic, onion powder, pepper, salt and oregano
3. Add peas, tomato and chicken
4. Add parmesan cheese and bake at 400 F for 8-10 minutes, remove and serve

FREND BREAD PIZZA

Serves: 1

Prep Time: 10 Minutes

Cook Time: 10 Minutes

Total Time: 20 Minutes

INGREDIENTS

- 1 loaf French bread
- pizza sauce
- mozzarella cheese
- salami

DIRECTIONS

1. Take a French bread and cut on half
2. Add pizza sauce, salami and top with mozzarella cheese
3. Bake in the convection oven for 10 minutes at 300 F
4. Remove and serve

TROUT FILLET PACKETS

Serves: **4**

Prep Time: **10** Minutes

Cook Time: **30** Minutes

Total Time: **40** Minutes

INGREDIENTS

- 3 springs parsley
- 1 lemon
- 2 trout fillets
- salt
- pepper
- 1 garlic clove
- 1-ounce butter

DIRECTIONS

1. Rinse parsley, pluck leaves and chop finely
2. Rinse lemon in hot water and wipe dry
3. Cut 3-4 slices of lemon
4. Rinse trout fillets and pat dry, season with salt and pepper
5. Mash garlic and mix with butter in a bowl, add parsley and stir to combine
6. Place in a baking dish and bake at 400 F for 10-12 minutes, remove and serve

GARLIC CHICKEN WITH HERBS

Serves: 4

Prep Time: *20* Minutes

Cook Time: *60* Minutes

Total Time: *80* Minutes

INGREDIENTS

- 3 boneless chicken breast

MARINADE

- 1 tablespoon olive oil

- 1 tablespoon herbs de Provence
- 1 tablespoon garlic powder

DIRECTIONS

1. In a bowl mix all marinade ingredients
2. Brush on the skin of chicken breast and arrange on a cooking sheet, allow to sit for 5-10 minutes
3. Preheat convection oven at 350 F and bake for 50 minutes, remove and serve

PIZZA WITH BRUSSELS SPROUTS

Serves: **2**
Prep Time: **20** Minutes
Cook Time: **30** Minutes
Total Time: **50** Minutes

INGREDIENTS

- 6-sounces rye flour
- 3 tsp olive oil
- 2 tsp tomato paste

- pepper
- salt
- brown sugar
- 4-ounces quark
- 1 lb. Brussels sprouts
- 1 garlic glove
- 1 spring marjoram
- 2-ounces mozzarella
- 6-ounces diced tomatoes

DIRECTIONS

1. Prepare pizza dough by mixing flour, sugar, salt using a mixed
2. Add water, oil and quark while mixing
3. Rinse Brussel sprouts, remove leaves, peel garlic and chop finely
4. Drain the mozzarella and cut into slices
5. Mix tomatoes with tomato pate and add marjoram, season with pepper and salt and spread over the dough
6. Distribute mozzarella and sauce and top with Brussels sprouts and sprinkle garlic and pine nuts over the pizza
7. Bake in convection oven at 375 F for 15-20 minutes
8. Remove and serve

SALAMI PIZZA

Serves: **4**

Prep Time: **10** Minutes

Cook Time: **20** Minutes

Total Time: **30** Minutes

INGREDIENTS

- 2 cups flour
- ½ cup pizza sauce
- salami
- toppings of choice
- 1 tablespoon baking powder
- 1 tsp salt
- 3 tablespoons butter
- 1 cup milk
- 1 cup mozzarella cheese

DIRECTIONS

1. **Preheat convection oven to 375 F**
2. **Microwave butter for 30 seconds, add flour, salt, baking powder and one cup of milk**
3. **Mix until well combined**

4. Brush a pan with melted butter
5. Brush the dough with butter and place in the pan
6. Add salami, mozzarella, pepperoni, pizza sauce, or any other topping
7. Bake for 12-15 minutes or until golden brown
8. Remove and serve

LOW CARB PIZZA

Serves: 2
Prep Time: **10** Minutes
Cook Time: **10** Minutes
Total Time: **20** Minutes

INGREDIENTS

- 1 low carb tortilla
- 16-pieces pepperoni
- 1 tablespoon pizza sauce
- ½ cup mozzarella shredded
- 1 tsp vegetable oil
- ½ lb. Italian sausage
- ½ cup green pepper
- ½ onion

DIRECTIONS

1. Preheat convection oven to 400 F
2. In a skillet add oil over medium heat
3. Spoon on pizza sauce on tortilla and spread, add pepperoni, green pepper, onion, mozzarella
4. Bake for 10-12 minutes, remove and serve

VEGAN PORTOBELLO PIZZA

Serves: 2
Prep Time: 10 Minutes
Cook Time: 10 Minutes
Total Time: 20 Minutes

INGREDIENTS

- 1 gluten free tortilla
- 1 cup Portobello mushrooms
- 1 tablespoon Kalamata olives
- parmesan cheese
- ½ cup parmesan hummus

- ¼ cup arugula
- ½ cup onion

DIRECTIONS

1. Preheat convection oven to 375 F (also this recipe can be done in a *toaster oven*)
2. Spread hummus, onion, mushrooms, arugula and olives
3. Sprinkle with parmesan cheese
4. Bake pizza for 8-10 minutes or until golden brown
5. Remove and serve

ZUCCHINI PIZZA

Serves: 2
Prep Time: 10 Minutes
Cook Time: 15 Minutes
Total Time: 25 Minutes

INGREDIENTS

- 1 lemon
- 4 springs marjoram

- pizza dough
- 8-ounces mozzarella
- 1 zucchini
- salt
- 4 tsp olive oil
- pepper
- 2 garlic gloves

DIRECTIONS

1. Grate zucchini on a box grater and sprinkle salt, set aside
2. In a bowl mix lemon zest, olive oil, lemon juice and grated zucchini
3. In another bowl mix marjoram, olive oil and garlic
4. On a baking sheet transfer pizza dough, a sprinkle with marjoram and garlic oil
5. Spread zucchini over the pizzas
6. Cut mozzarella into pieces and layer on top of the zucchini
7. Bake at 400 F for 20 minutes
8. Remove and sprinkle with marjoram before serving

GLUTEN FREE PIZZA

Serves: *1*

Prep Time: *10* Minutes

Cook Time: *20* Minutes

Total Time: *30* Minutes

INGREDIENTS

- 1 package nitrate free salami
- 1 large bushel basil
- black pepper
- 1 tablespoon olive oil
- 1 can tomato paste
- 6 oz. mozzarella cheese
- 2 ripe tomatoes

CRUST

- 1 package gluten free pizza crust mix
- 1 cup water
- 1 egg
- 1 tablespoon olive oil
- 1 packet dry yeast

DIRECTIONS

1. Prepare gluten free pizza dough using the ingredients from CRUST
2. Drizzle olive oil on top and spread tomato paste
3. Top with salami, sliced tomato, mozzarella and basil
4. Bake at 400 F for 15-20 minutes or until golden brown
5. Remove and serve

SOUS VIDE EGGS BENEDICT PIZZA

Serves: 2
Prep Time: 10 Minutes
Cook Time: 15 Minutes
Total Time: 25 Minutes

INGREDIENTS

- pizza dough
- 2 slices bacon
- 1 oz. hollandaise sauce
- parsley
- 2 sous vide eggs
- 2,7 oz. mozzarella

DIRECTIONS

1. Set water at 170 F and drop eggs, cook for 10-12 minutes and transfer to cold water, set aside
2. Stretch dough as much as possible and dust with flour
3. Distribute mozzarella, bacon and bake in convection oven for 1-2 minutes
4. Crack sous vide eggs, in a bowl and place them on top of pizza
5. Season with salt and pepper
6. Bake at 400F for 10-12 minutes
7. Remove and drizzle Hollandaise sauce over eggs and serve

TUNA PIZZA

Serves: *4*
Prep Time: *10* Minutes
Cook Time: *30* Minutes
Total Time: *40* Minutes

INGREDIENTS

- pizza dough

- salt
- pepper
- 10 black olives
- ½ bunch basil
- ½ lemon
- ½ cup tomato sauce
- 3 tomatoes
- 2 dried oregano
- 4 ounces canned tuna

DIRECTIONS

1. Spread tomato pate over pizza dough
2. Cut tomato into sliced and place them over pizza dough
3. Season with salt, oregano, pepper
4. Bake at 400 F for 10-12 minutes
5. Remove pizza and add basil, tuna and olive, season with lemon juice and serve

ARUGULA PIZZA

Serves: **1**

Prep Time: **10** Minutes

Cook Time: **10** Minutes

Total Time: **20** Minutes

INGREDIENTS

- Pizza dough
- balsamic vinegar
- parmesan cheese
- Handful of arugula
- 3 vine ripened tomatoes
- ½ onion
- 2 oz. mozzarella
- 1 oz. tomato sauce

DIRECTIONS

1. Preheat oven to 450 F
2. Stretch pizza dough and add mozzarella, bake for 1-2 minutes
3. Remove and top with arugula, onions, tomatoes, parmesan cheese and season with salt

4. Cook for another 6-8 minutes at 200 F
5. Remove and serve

ENGLISH MUFFIN PIZZAS

Serves: **12**

Prep Time: **10** Minutes

Cook Time: **10** Minutes

Total Time: **20** Minutes

INGREDIENTS

- 1 cup pizza sauce
- 1 can olives
- 1 package pepperoni slices
- 12 English muffins
- 1 cup cheddar cheese
- 1 cup mozzarella cheese

DIRECTIONS

1. Preheat convection oven to 325 F

2. Slice English muffins in half and lay down on a baking sheet
3. Spread pizza sauce on each muffin and sprinkle with shredded cheese
4. Add olives, cheddar cheese, mozzarella cheese, pepperoni
5. Bake for 10-12 minutes or until golden brown
6. Remove and serve

CHIKEN PIZZA WITH GOAT CHEESE

Serves: 2
Prep Time: 10 Minutes
Cook Time: 15 Minutes
Total Time: 25 Minutes

INGREDIENTS

- Pizza dough
- 1 cup cranberry sauce
- 1 cup chicken
- 2 oz. goat cheese
- ¼ cup walnuts
- 1 tsp rosemary

DIRECTIONS

1. Preheat convection oven to 400 F
2. Stretch pizza dough and bake pizza dough for 4-6 minutes
3. Remove and spread cranberry sauce all over the dough, top with chicken, walnuts, goat cheese, and bake again for another 10-12 minutes
4. Remove pizza and sprinkle with rosemary and serve

ONION BACON PIZZA

Serves: **2**

Prep Time: **10** Minutes

Cook Time: **20** Minutes

Total Time: **30** Minutes

INGREDIENTS

- 1 whole wheat pizza dough
- 1 onion
- 1 tablespoon olive oil
- 1 lb. mozzarella cheese

- 5 oz. bacon

DIRECTIONS

1. Preheat convection oven to 400 F
2. In a cast iron skillet add onions and olive oil and cook until caramelized for 5-6 minutes
3. Place dough on flat surface
4. Place the cheese over pizza dough, onions and bacon
5. Bake the pizza in the convection oven for 20 minutes or until done, remove and serve

POLENTA PIZZA

Serves: 2
Prep Time: 10 Minutes
Cook Time: 20 Minutes
Total Time: 30 Minutes

INGREDIENTS

- salt
- 3-ounces polenta
- nutmeg

- pepper
- 2 tablespoons sour cream
- 2 tomatoes
- 2 slices salami
- 2 corn canned
- 1 ball mozzarella

DIRECTIONS

1. In a pot boil water with salt and stir in polenta, nutmeg and season with pepper
2. Cook polenta on low heat, stir in sour cream and season
3. Remove polenta on a baking sheet let it cool and create a 20-30 cm circle
4. Add tomatoes, salami, corn, mozzarella and distribute over polenta pizza
5. Bake in convection oven at 350 F for 15-20 minutes or until golden brown
6. Remove and serve

DINNER

FILO-WRAPPED BRIE

Serves: **8**

Prep Time: **10** Minutes

Cook Time: **40** Minutes

Total Time: **50** Minutes

INGREDIENTS

- ¼ cup pine nuts
- 2 tablespoons melted butter
- 3 sheets filo dough
- ½ cup dried tomatoes

DIRECTIONS

1. Place nuts in a pie pan and bake at 325 F in a convection oven until golden brown
2. In a bowl chop tomatoes and mix with oil, add also butter
3. Cut filo sheets and brush them with butter mixture
4. Spread toasted nuts, basil, chopped tomatoes on filo stack and place cheese on top of tomato mixture

5. Brush with butter mixture and place in a pie pan, bake for 25-30 minutes in the convection oven at 325 F
6. Remove and serve

LAMB SHANKS WITH CAPERS

Serves: **6**

Prep Time: **10** Minutes

Cook Time: **240** Minutes

Total Time: **250** Minutes

INGREDIENTS

- 5 lamb shanks
- 1 cup green olives
- ½ cup rosemary leaves
- 1 bottle dry white wine
- 1 tsp pepper
- 1 tsp lemon peel
- 2 tablespoons lemon juice
- 1 jar capers

DIRECTIONS

1. Rinse lamb and pat dry, lay shanks in a pan and bake at 425 F for 25-30 minutes
2. In a strainer add olives and capers and rinse with water
3. Scatter capers, rosemary and olives over lamb and add wine
4. Sprinkle pepper over the meat and lemon juice
5. Bake until meat is tender for 3-4 hours
6. Remove from oven, garnish with ½ cup watercress springs and serve

SICILIAN STRATA

Serves: 8
Prep Time: 10 Minutes
Cook Time: 50 Minutes
Total Time: 60 Minutes

INGREDIENTS

- 1 loaf Italian bread
- 2 cups milk
- ½ cup sliced green onions

- ½ cup parmesan cheese
- 1 can chopped tomatoes
- ½ cup black olives
- 1 tsp Italian seasoning
- ½ tsp salt
- ¼ tsp pepper
- ½ cup parsley
- 2 tablespoons capers
- 3-ounces prosciutto
- ½ cup canned red peppers
- ½ cup mozzarella cheese
- 5 eggs

DIRECTIONS

1. In a baking dish spread half the bread cubes, top with peppers, parmesan cheese, prosciutto, green olives, spread remaining bread cubes on top, then add olives, mozzarella and tomatoes
2. In a bowl whisk salt, pepper, eggs, Italian seasoning, milk and blend, pour over ingredients
3. Bake at 350 F in a convection oven for 45-50 minutes, sprinkle with parsley and capers, remove and serve

SPICED TURKEY PICNIC LOAF

Serves: **4**

Prep Time: **10** Minutes

Cook Time: **50** Minutes

Total Time: **60** Minutes

INGREDIENTS

- 6-ounces mushrooms
- ¼ tsp salt
- ¼ tsp allspice
- ¼ tsp cinnamon
- 1 tablespoon molasses
- ¼ cup all-purpose flour
- 1 lb. turkey
- ¼ cup chicken broth
- 1 egg
- 5 slices prosciutto
- 1 onion
- 2 tablespoons salad oil
- ¼ tsp cayenne
- 2 tablespoons cider
- ¼ tsp nutmeg

- 2/4 cup drained cocktail onions

DIRECTIONS

1. In a pan, stir mushrooms, onion and cook for 5-10 minutes
2. Add cayenne, cinnamon, nutmeg, allspice, stir for for 2-3 minutes, add molasses, vinegar and stir until liquid is evaporated
3. In a bowl add flour and mix to blend, add turkey, broth, egg and mix well, stir in pickled onions
4. In a loaf pan, line a layer f prosciutto sliced, scrape meat mixture into pan and bake turkey loaf at 325 F for about 50 minutes
5. When ready, remove and serve

ROAST TURKEY

Serves: *4*

Prep Time: *10* Minutes

Cook Time: *30* Minutes

Total Time: *40* Minutes

INGREDIENTS

- melted butter
- 1 turkey
- classic gravy

DIRECTIONS

1. Remove leg truss from turkey, remove giblets and save for classic gravy
2. Rinse turkey inside and out, pat dry and rub with butter
3. Place turkey in a roasting pan, insert a thermometer and roast in a convection oven until thermometer registers 160
4. Transfer turkey to a platter, let it cool for 20 minutes, cut drumsticks from thighs and bake them at 425 for 12-15 minutes, remove and serve

PECAN BALLS

Serves: **24**
Prep Time: **10** Minutes
Cook Time: **30** Minutes
Total Time: **40** Minutes

INGREDIENTS

- 1 cu butter
- ½ tsp baking powder
- 1 cup pecans
- 1 cup powdered sugar
- 1 tsp vanilla
- 1 cup all-purpose flour

DIRECTIONS

1. In a bowl mix butter, vanilla, powdered sugar until smooth
2. In another bowl mix baking powder, flour and add mixture to the butter mixture and mix well, stir in pecans
3. Shape dough into 1 inch balls and place on baking sheets
4. Bake at 325 F for 20 minutes, when ready remove and serve with powdered sugar

ROASTED FISH

Serves: 4
Prep Time: 10 Minutes
Cook Time: 30 Minutes
Total Time: 40 Minutes

INGREDIENTS

- 4 pieces skinned halibut
- 1 tablespoon sliced chives
- 4-ounces fresh shiitake mushrooms
- 1 tablespoon minced garlic
- ½ cup chicken broth
- 1 tablespoon olive oil
- salt
- ½ cup tomato sauce
- 1 cup soybeans
- kabocha coulis
- 1 tablespoon basil

DIRECTIONS

1. Coat fish with olive oil, sprinkle with pepper and place in a frying pan, cook for 1-2 minutes per side

2. Transfer to a convection oven and bake for 8-10 minutes at 325 F
3. Rinse and rain mushrooms, cut mushrooms into ½ inch chunks
4. In a frying pan over medium heat stir in mushrooms and garlic, add oil, mushrooms and cook for 5 minutes
5. Add tomato sauce, broth, soybeans, and cook until soybeans are tinder
6. On a plate add soybean mixture, top with fish, spoon kabocha coulis and garnish fish with remaining chives

GREEK PEACH PIE

Serves: 8

Prep Time: 10 Minutes

Cook Time: 50 Minutes

Total Time: 60 Minutes

INGREDIENTS

- 1 package cream cheese
- ½ cup cornstarch
- 5 cups sliced peaches

- ¾ cup orange juice
- ½ cup lemon juice
- 1 cup sugar

DIRECTIONS

1. Prick bottom and sides of unbaked pastry in a pan and bake at 350 F until golden brown
2. In a bowl mix sugar with cream cheese until smooth and spread over pastry
3. In a blender mix peaches, cornstarch, orange juice, sugar and pour mixture in a pan, stir over medium heat for 4-5 minutes, remove from heat and stir in lemon juice
4. Add remaining peaches and mix to coat, let it cool for 25-30 minutes and then scrape onto cream cheese mixture
5. Chill for a couple of hours and cut into wedges and serve

SPICED PECANS

Serves: **4**
Prep Time: **10** Minutes
Cook Time: **30** Minutes

Total Time: **40** Minutes

INGREDIENTS

- ½ cup sugar
- 1 egg
- ½ tsp cinnamon
- 1 cup pecan halves
- 2/4 tsp cayenne
- ¼ tsp salt
- ¼ tsp coriander
- ¼ tsp allspice
- 1 tsp vegetable oil

DIRECTIONS

1. In a bowl mix cayenne, salt, sugar, cinnamon, coriander, all spice and whisk in vegetable oil, egg and pecan halves
2. Spread mixture in a baking pan and bake at 300 F and cook for 25 minutes, remove and serve

BUTTERNUT SQUASH WITH TOMATOES

Serves: **4**

Prep Time: **10** Minutes

Cook Time: **120** Minutes

Total Time: **130** Minutes

INGREDIENTS

- 1 medium butternut squash
- 1 red chile
- 4 plum tomatoes
- 1-ounce ginger
- 1 clove garlic
- 1 tablespoon sugar
- salt/ pepper
- 2 tablespoons olive oil

LIME YOGURT

- ½ cup Greek yogurt
- ½ tsp cardamom
- zest f one lime
- 1 tsp lime juice

DIRECTIONS

1. Preheat the convection oven to 425 F
2. In a bowl mix salt, olive oil, squash and black pepper, spread the mixture on a baking sheet and roast for 35 minutes or until golden brown, remove from the convection oven and set aside
3. On a parchment-lined baking sheet place the tomatoes, sprinkle with salt and drizzle with oil, cook for 80 minutes
4. In a bowl mix garlic, chile, ginger, salt and pour over tomatoes, cook for another 30 minutes, remove and set aside
5. Mix all lime yogurt ingredients and keep in the fridge
6. For serving, spread the squash on a platter and layer the tomatoes in between, pour over lime yogurt and sprinkle with cilantro

MAYONNAISE ROASTED TURKEY

Serves: *12*

Prep Time: *10* Minutes

Cook Time: *150* Minutes

Total Time: *160* Minutes

INGREDIENTS

- 1 16 lbs. turkey
- 10 stems fresh thyme
- 1 stick salted butter
- 5 streams of oregano
- 1 jar mayonnaise
- ground pepper and salt
- 12 sage leaves
- 5 stalks celery
- 1 onion

DIRECTIONS

1. Preheat convection oven to 425 F
2. Scatter celery and onions on the bottom of the roasting pan
3. Remove the leaves from stems and mix with mayonnaise, turn the turkey over and rub herbs and mayonnaise mixture over the turkey, sprinkle salt and pepper
4. Roast for 30 minutes, and then lower the heat to 350 F and cook for 120 minutes
5. Remove from the convection oven and serve

BAKED SOWRDFISH

Serves: **4**

Prep Time: **10** Minutes

Cook Time: **30** Minutes

Total Time: **40** Minutes

INGREDIENTS

- 2 cloves garlic
- salt
- 3 swordfish steaks
- juice of 1 lemon
- 1 tablespoon leaf parsley
- 1 tablespoon olive oil

DIRECTIONS

1. Preheat convection oven to 325 F
2. In a skillet add garlic with olive oil and sprinkle with salt
3. Add the swordfish steaks and turn over so they are coated in the mixture
4. Bake for 20 minutes, add lemon juice and serve

BEEF MEATBALLS

Serves: *8*

Prep Time: *10* Minutes

Cook Time: *40* Minutes

Total Time: *50* Minutes

INGREDIENTS

- 2 lbs. beef meat
- 1 lb. pork
- 1 lb. ground pork fat
- 1 tablespoon cayenne
- 1 tablespoon pepper
- 1 tablespoon salt
- 1 tablespoon meat seasoning
- 1 tablespoon paprika
- ½ tsp sugar
- 1 cup breadcrumbs
- 1-quart chicken stock

DIRECTIONS

1. **Preheat convection oven to 325 F**

2. In a bowl mix all ingredients except the chicken stock and set aside
3. Form into small meat balls and place them in a baking dish and fill with chicken stock
4. Bake for 40 minutes, remove and serve

SALMON FILLETS

Serves: 6
Prep Time: 10 Minutes
Cook Time: 30 Minutes
Total Time: 40 Minutes

INGREDIENTS

- 4 salmon fillets
- salt
- lemon wedge
- 1 tsp dried dill weed
- 1 tsp lemon pepper

DIRECTIONS

1. Sprinkle salt over the salmon fillets
2. Place the fillets in a baking dish and add dill weed
3. Bake for 30 minute in the convection oven or until done at 275 F
4. Remove and serve with with lemon wedge and lemon pepper

ROASTED MEAT AND VEGETABLES

Serves: **6**

Prep Time: **10** Minutes

Cook Time: **35** Minutes

Total Time: **45** Minutes

INGREDIENTS

- 6 eggs
- 1 tablespoon flour
- salt
- nutmeg
- 1 onion
- 1 tablespoon parmesan cheese
- butter
- 1 cup shredded cheese

- 1 cup milk
- 1 cup vegetable mix
- 1 cup meat

DIRECTIONS

1. Preheat the convection oven to 425 F
2. In a skillet add oil, garlic, vegetables, meat and cook for 2-3 minutes then remove and set aside
3. In a bowl mix eggs, flour, cheese and milk
4. Add the onion mixture, salt and pepper
5. In a pan pour the contents of the bowl and sprinkle with parmesan cheese and nutmeg
6. Place the dish in the convection oven and bake for 30-35 minutes or until done, remove and serve

CHEDDAR BACON EXPLOSION

Serves: 6

Prep Time: 10 Minutes

Cook Time: 30 Minutes

Total Time: 40 Minutes

INGREDIENTS

- 30 slices bacon
- 2 cups shredded cheese
- 4 cups spinach
- 1 tablespoon chipotle seasoning
- 1 tsp Mrs. Dash table seasoning

DIRECTIONS

1. Preheat convection oven to 350 F
2. Place bacon down and make sure all are facing the same way half vertical and half horizontal
3. Season with seasoning, add cheese and top with spinach and using your hands compress the spinach
4. Roll tight like a cigarette, preferably compressed as much as possible
5. Season it out the outside, add salt and place it in the oven for 60 minutes
6. When ready remove and let it cool before serving

FRENCH TOAST

Serves: 4
Prep Time: 10 Minutes

Cook Time: **10** Minutes

Total Time: **20** Minutes

INGREDIENTS

- 3 slices bread
- 1-quart heavy cream
- 1 cup sugar
- 3 eggs
- 1 cup vegetable oil
- powdered sugar
- maple syrup

DIRECTIONS

1. Preheat convection oven to 325 F
2. Warm heavy cream with sugar and pour over bread and allow to soak for 4-5 minutes
3. In a pan add oil over medium heat and whisk sugar with the eggs
4. Dredge each piece of bread in egg mixture and place into pan, cook 1-2 minutes per side
5. Transfer to a plate, dust with powdered sugar and serve with maple syrup

ROASTED BACON

Serves: 2
Prep Time: 10 Minutes
Cook Time: 10 Minutes
Total Time: 20 Minutes

INGREDIENTS

- 10 slices bacon

DIRECTIONS

1. Preheat convection oven to 375 F
2. Like a sheet pan with a sheet of aluminum foil and place bacon on sheet
3. Bake for 20 minutes, remove and serve

THANK YOU FOR READING THIS BOOK!

Made in the USA
Middletown, DE
12 June 2020